The 16-Word Sales Letter™

*A proven method of writing
multi-million-dollar copy faster
than you ever thought possible*

By Evaldo Albuquerque

Copyright © 2019 Evaldo Albuquerque.

ALL RIGHTS RESERVED

This book or any portion thereof may not be reproduced or used in any manner whatsoever without the express written permission of the copyright owner and publisher except for the use of brief quotations in a book review.

Edited by

Ryan R.

Cover art by

Chris Hunter

Advanced Praise for
The 16-Word Sales Letter™

*"**This is the book I've been waiting for.** For years, I've been asking myself: How can a guy whose native language is not even English be one of the best U.S. copywriters in history? Now I have the answer... nicely reduced to a simple, understandable formula. And the best thing is that it's a usable formula. Anyone seriously interested in copywriting should discover Evaldo's secret."*

—Bill Bonner, Founder Agora Inc.

"It's not often that I come upon a copywriting strategy that feels new to me. And even less frequently do I encounter one that is both new and exciting. Evaldo Albuquerque's "16 Word Sales Letter™" is such a strategy. **I'm going to recommend this as a must-read to all my copywriting proteges.**"*

—Mark Ford, best-selling author and chief growth strategist for Agora, Inc.

*"**Evaldo is the world's greatest copywriter you've never heard of.** Why haven't you heard of him? Because while others are self-promoting ... heck, while they're eating, sleeping and relaxing... he's cranking out the next blockbuster. He never stops. He's a 9-figure sales machine and our business's secret weapon. This book is your blueprint to how the machine dominates. Read it and put it into action. Your royalty check will thank you."*

—Peter Coyne, founder of Paradigm Press, Agora Financial's largest imprint

3

"I'm recommending this book to everyone in my company, and making it required reading for all new hires. When it comes to books on "writing" I try to read everything new, and no matter how many books I pick up, I rarely find any ideas that are innovative (or even useful), but **this book shattered my expectations—I found page after page packed with fresh ideas.** *It's engaging to read, and very easy to implement the writing techniques.*

"Evaldo has uncovered a new way to write sales copy that is perfect for today's buyers; I really love this book, and after you turn the first two pages, you'll see exactly why. **It's a must-read primer for anyone who writes sales copy.... Read this book—and learn from one of the best."**

—Oren Klaff, best-selling author of Pitch Anything
and Flip the Script

"Few people know his name. Yet, those at the highest levels of direct response advertising consider Evaldo Albuquerque the Michael Jordan of modern financial copywriting. *His new book, The 16 Word Sales Letter™, reveals for the first time the secret to his astonishing success. In split tests, the selling formula Evaldo reveals in his book has won, repeatedly, against ad copy written by the world's top copywriters. When asked at a recent seminar I gave what are the two best books I've ever read on copywriting, my answer was Breakthrough Advertising by Eugene Schwartz and The 16 Word Sales Letter™ by Evaldo Albuquerque."*

—Caleb O'Dowd, www.roitips.com

Table of Contents

Foreword

The Power of Just 16 Little Words...

(and how those words can change your future, forever)

Can a short sentence change the history of the world?

And more importantly, can those same words change *your* fate... *your* destiny... *your* future?

To answer, we simply have to go back to a steamy day in Houston, TX more than 50 years ago...

SETTING: RICE STADIUM, Houston, Texas, 81 degrees

DATE: September 12, 1962

CHARACTERS: John F. Kennedy, Jr... and 40,000 packed fans (many of whom, children.)

In front of a filled stadium Kennedy muttered these now famous 10 words...

"We choose to go to the Moon in this decade..."

10. Short. Words.

And America was changed, forever...

As you may remember from history class, America was losing the race to space badly at the time. The Soviets were dominating.

Kennedy knew he needed to persuade the nation with his desire to "put a man on the moon."

So he (and his speechwriters, no doubt) went to work on his act of persuasion... eventually coming up with the 10 words you've just read.

Now, although the sentence was short, the rhetoric packed in those 10 words whallowed the trajectory of the nation.

John Jordan, author of "Kennedy's Romantic Moon and Its Rhetorical Legacy for Space Exploration" explains the three techniques Kennedy used to move America to act...

> *"[Kennedy's speech used] a characterization of space as a beckoning frontier; an articulation of time that locates the endeavor within a historical moment of urgency and plausibility; and a final, cumulative strategy that invites audience members to live up to their pioneering heritage by going to the Moon."*

Just over seven years later, Apollo 11 touched down on the gray, sandy surface of the moon. Neil and Buzz took their famous walk outside and planted the American flag.

And now, think about how much space technology touches your life everyday...

From Google Earth imagery of your house... to the GPS you enjoy in your car... to listening to SIRIUS satellite radio...

Would it all have been possible without Kennedy's 10 words?

**Now, back to you... and the reason you're reading this book...
which surely ISN'T for a history lesson...**

To transition to *your* story, I need to take you to a wholly different, much colder setting...

SETTING: Agora Financial offices in Baltimore, MD

DATE: February 1st, 2019

CHARACTERS: Me (Joe Schriefer) and the author of this book (Evaldo)

And this story starts with a question. Or, rather, a list of questions...

"How do you do it?" I asked Evaldo.

"Do what?," he quipped back.

"How does a Brazilian man... whose native language is Portuguese... crush every single American copywriter that I've ever seen?"

To put the question in context, at Agora Financial we eat, live and sleep copywriting. In my part in helping to run the business I've personally worked with more than 100+ copywriters...

... Many of which are the "A-list" copywriters you've come to know...

And none of them... NONE of them... could hold a proverbial candle to the year that Evaldo has just had.

Just a decade before I met Evaldo he only knew a basic few English words -- like "book," "cat", and "table."

Yet in 2018 alone he (somehow) managed to bring in more than 100,000 front end customers AND write more than $80,000,000 worth of backend sales copy.

And to put those numbers in perspective...

They were more than 6 times more revenue I'd ever seen ANYONE produce.

Said a different way, 600% more than any "A-list" writer I'd ever worked with.

And Evaldo wasn't even a native English speaker!

I had to know his "secret..."

"C'mon, Evaldo, you're doing something differently than anyone I've ever met," I started to ask again. *"Spill it... what's the secret."*

"It all comes down to 16 simple words..." he said in his (still thick) accent.

As we spent the rest of the day together, he walked me through his secret "16-word sales letter™."

It's a strategy I'd never seen before in any of the copywriting guru courses...

A totally brand new breakthrough that allows you to tap into your customer's core belief, persuade that customer, and influence action.

Just like JFK muttered 10 words that put a man on the moon, you, too, can use Evaldo's 16 words to alter your copywriting future... your financial future... forever.

Read this book. Memorize these 16 words. Use Evaldo's system in your next sales letter.

Then, just weeks later...

Watch in amazement as these 16 words add dollars to your bank account.

Best of all, it's so simple to execute that ANYONE can do it...

... Even a Brazilian man... who doesn't speak native English... Who invented a system that turned himself into America's #1 copywriter.

Sincerely,

Joe Schriefer

Publisher, Agora Financial

Introduction

"...Baby One More Time" (Britney Spears), "I Kissed a Girl" (Katy Perry), "One More Night" (Maroon 5), "Shake It Off" (Taylor Swift), "Can't Feel My Face" (The Weeknd), "Can't Stop the Feeling!" (Justin Timberlake).

What do all these songs have in common?

Two things. First, they all hit #1 on the Billboard Hot 100 list. Second, believe it or not, they were all written by the same man: Max Martin. This guy has his hands in countless blockbuster pop songs of the last two decades. With 22 number one singles in the U.S., he's catching up with John Lennon (26) and Paul McCartney (32) as the most successful songwriter in Billboard chart history.

What's even more interesting is that, unlike John Lennon and Paul McCartney, Max Martin writes songs for a diverse range of artists, from the Backstreet Boys to Rhianna to Bon Jovi. And English isn't his first language: he's Swedish.

Some of his lyrics don't even quite make sense. And yet, it seems everything he touches turns into a major hit. His songs just strike an emotional chord with people and make them want to sing along.

What do all his songs have in common? First, they have short unique intro, a kind of a pattern interrupt. When you listen to his songs, you'll recognize it right off the bat.

Max explains that he "came from the DJ world.... [T]o keep people on the floor, they had to know what was the song right away." A great example of this is the opening to Britney Spears's "...Baby One More Time" with its immediately recognizable "DUN DUN DUN."

Second, all of Max's songs hit the chorus within a minute, and often much faster. Why? Because today's audience has a much shorter attention span than audiences of the past. Max's songs get to the point fast, before people have a chance to switch the station.

Third, his lyrics are written in very, very basic English. Most are well below a fourth-grade reading level. His songs also have simple harmonic structure, mainly 3 to 4 chords.

And finally, they develop slowly, introducing one new sound or instrument at a time. He doesn't overwhelm the listener with too much at the same time. And he uses those different elements to create tension and balance.

If you're a copywriter like myself or work in direct marketing, you can see some parallels between what Max does with music and some basic principles of copywriting. I'm sure there's a lot more to his formula for success.

After all, I'm no musician. I can't play a single instrument. But my point is, this guy has definitely figured something out. As a copywriter, I'm intrigued. Because at the end of the day, much like movies and songs, sales letters also try to touch people on an emotional level.

If Max Martin has figured out a formula for success, could there also be a secret formula for sales letters that would virtually guarantee success? That's the question I've been trying to answer for the past few years. After years of studying copy that converts, reading books on persuasion techniques, and most important, writing many, many, many sales letters that were total failures... I think I finally found it.

Before finding this formula, I was selling an average of about $2-3 million a year. Nothing spectacular. I was an average copywriter who had a "hit ratio" of about 20%-40%. Meaning, for every five sales letter I wrote, only one or two would work.

That meant I spent most of my time writing bombs that made me no royalties. But I did gain something that's worth way more than a fat royalty check. Those bombs helped me find the right direction. They showed me what works. And what doesn't.

After so much trial and error, I developed a simple formula... one so simple that it can be explained in just 16 words. In theory, it made a lot of sense to me. But I had no idea if it would work.

When I first used it in early 2017 in a video sales letter I was working on, I wasn't expecting much.

What happened next blew me away....

Chapter 1

The 16-Word Sales Letter™ that Sold $120+ Million in Two years

That VSL went live on July 2017. Within an hour, sales started to pour in. And they haven't stopped yet, as I write this in 2019.

So far, that single piece of copy that followed the formula has generated more than $30 million in sales. After that blockbuster, I was hooked. Who wouldn't be?

All I have to do is follow this 16-word method and I can sell millions? Count me in! I started using this formula in every single project I wrote. As a result, my copy has generated over $120 million in just two years, from several different offers, different products, and different ideas. The one constant was this formula.

My "hit ratio" went from 20-30% to 60%-80%.

Now, before you assume I'm some sort of copy genius, you should know that when I was 21 years old, I knew only a few words in English, words like "book," "cat," "dog," and "table." No joke. A decade ago I didn't even know what copywriting was. When I started writing copy in 2013, I had zero training in direct marketing—or any kind of marketing, for that matter.

So if this works for me, I know it can work for anyone.

Yes, even if you're a complete newbie. How do I know? Because as soon as I started mentoring other copywriters and applying my method to their copy, many of them went from zero to multi-million-dollar sales, seemingly out of the blue. One guy (I'll call him Mike) wrote me to say:

"Before I worked with Evaldo, I knew squat about copywriting. Nothing. I had made zero dollars writing persuasive copy.

"Within five months, my very first sales letter generated over $5 million in sales. I couldn't believe it. I knew my life would never be the same.

"The copywriting strategies and concepts Evaldo taught me have forever altered the direction of my life and career, and ensured my future prosperity as a professional copywriter."

Another guy, I'll call him Justin, says:

"Before I started working with Evaldo, I was just a 23-year old college dropout with no prospects and less than $200 to my name.

"Two years later, and I'm making 6-figures a year, working when and where I want.

"While all the copywriting 'gurus' are at seminars talking about hypothetical, theoretical bullshit... Evaldo is sitting in the corner with his laptop, writing tens of millions of dollars in winning copy every single year."

Brian (also an alias) also sent me a "thank you" note, saying:

"It's crazy to think... this year I'll take home 10 times more money than I made last year. I paid off $30k in student loans in one lump sum payment.... Now I'm looking for a new house to buy!

"Working with Evaldo is the closest thing to guaranteeing a multi-million dollar promotion EVERY TIME you put a campaign together.

"This might sound ridiculous... But if I had the choice of ANY mentor in the history of copywriting (Gary Halbert, Gene Schwartz, Gary Bencivenga)... I would choose Evaldo Albuquerque. The results speak for themselves... I've got $20mm+ in sales with a little more than a year of copywriting experience."

Yeah, I know... Brian has lost his mind for comparing me to those copy legends. But holy shit... Isn't that amazing?

So What's the Secret 16-Word Sales Letter™?

Here it is:

"The secret to converting copy is to define the one belief, then answer these ten questions."

That's it. I'll make it even easier for you to remember. Just four words: One belief. Ten questions.

The one belief will not only help you judge the strength of your idea. It will also set the tone of your entire copy, the common thread that keeps everything together.

The ten questions will add a ton of emotional triggers to your copy. And since they're sequential, they will also help you organize your promo from lead all the way to the closing.

The beauty here is that these questions never change. Once you internalize them, writing a sales letter will become automatic for you. Follow this process, and staring at a blank

The 16-Word Sales Letter™

page for hours not knowing what to write next will become a thing of the past.

You'll also never get lost in the middle of the project. I know that for newbie copywriters, that's probably one of the biggest challenges they face. I know because I've been there. It's easy to get lost in the woods when you don't have a map pointing you in the right direction.

Imagine how much easier writing copy will become once you know exactly what to write, even before you type your first word. Your productivity will skyrocket. You know that means for you?

If you own a business, once you share this with your copywriters, you'll have no shortage of sales letters. This could help explode your business. If you're a copywriter like myself, it means more royalties! And more time to do whatever the heck you want!

I'm telling you this because that's exactly what happened to me. I used to write one full package every two months, which is average. After implementing this method, I was writing one new sales letter a month.

That's right. My productivity doubled. Using this method, I've written full packages in as little as two weeks... including a crypto offer that went on to bring in 100,000+ new paid names (before it "broke the Internet" and got banned on Google and other networks).

People around the office in Agora started asking me "how the hell do you crank out so much copy?" Some people thought I must be working 20 hours a day. But the truth is, I wasn't working harder. I was just working smarter.

So how does it work?

It all begins with the one belief.

Chapter 2

Your Mission: Make the Reader Believe in the One Belief

Before the 1980s, military plans used to be extremely robust, including every single detail imaginable. What each unit will do. What equipment they'll use. How they'll replace ammunition. And so on.

There was just one problem. The plans often became useless a few minutes into battle. As Mike Tyson has said, "Everyone has a plan, until they get punched in the mouth."

As you can imagine, a lot of unpredictable things happen in the battlefield. And when they do, everything you planned becomes useless.

After so many failed missions, the U.S. Army adapted its strategy and invented a concept called Commander's Intent (CI). It appears on top of every order specifying the desired end state of the operation (the goal).

Instead of being a play-by-play instruction manual, the CI provides only the desired destination. It gives everyone on the team the flexibility they need to react to unpredictable events. As Jocko Willink and Leif Babin write in their excellent book *Extreme Ownership*, about Navy SEAL leadership:

"While a simple statement, the Commander's Intent is actually the most important part of the brief. When understood by everyone involved in the execution of the plan, it guides each decision and action on the ground."

When you write a sales letter, you also must have a Commander's Intent. And that's exactly what "the one belief" is. It describes the ultimate goal of the sales letter.

When most people write copy, they don't have a mission. But how are you supposed to write copy that converts if you don't know the ultimate goal of the letter? How are you supposed to succeed if you don't know what you're trying to accomplish?

It's impossible. And it's a big reason why a lot of copywriters fail. It's a big reason why I've failed many times.

With the one belief, you will know what your mission is. It's your North Star, guiding you all the way to a high-converting sales letter.

Officers arrive at the Commander's Intent by asking themselves the question "What is the single most important thing we must do during the mission?" And that's how we arrive at the one belief.

The single most important thing you can do when you write a sales letter is to make the reader believe that:

This **new opportunity** is the key to **their desire** and it's only attainable through **my new mechanism**.

That's your mission. Write it down.

I learned this from Rich Schefren, who called this "the core concept." As Rich said, "If your Core Concept is accepted - buying your product, service, or whatever else becomes the next logical (and emotional) decision."

Later, Russel Brunson (who also learned this from Rich) wrote about it. He said: "If I can get someone to TRULY believe that the new opportunity is the key to what they want the most, and they can only get it through my vehicle, then they have no other options but to buy."

While Russel was talking about launching your business online, this concept can easily be applied to every single sales letter you write. It's a critical part of my formula.

The one belief will force you to find the core of your idea. It will force you to get rid of superfluous stuff and less important insights. As a result, you'll focus on the one idea that will drive your sales letter.

As you can see, you can break the one belief down into three main elements: the new opportunity, your prospect's desire, and the new mechanism. Let's dig deeper into each one.

The New Opportunity

Remember when I said the one belief will help you judge the strength of your idea? If you can't identify the new opportunity, then your idea isn't unique. And that means it's not even worth testing.

For example, "eating healthy and exercising" cannot be your new opportunity. Neither can "investing in the stock market." There's nothing unique about those ideas.

The new opportunity is what makes your idea unique, your unique selling proposition (USP). If you don't have one, your idea is worthless, as I'll prove to you in the next chapter.

But here's the thing. If your idea is truly unique, then your prospect will have no idea they need it, right? That's why it's not enough just to have something that's new.

In the sales letter, we also need to show why they need it. That's where their desires come in. They must believe that the new opportunity you're presenting is the key to their desire.

If they don't believe that, your new opportunity won't touch them on an emotional level. And it will be extremely hard for you to persuade your prospect.

Your Prospect Desire

The main thing here is to remember that your new opportunity can be the key to their desire only if it provides benefits. It can be the key to their desire only if it will help your prospect feel more significant, respected, and valued. If it can help increase your prospect's mental, physical, social, emotional, sexual, or financial well-being. Or if it can decrease or eliminate the risk of events that will negatively impact your prospect's mental, physical, social, emotional, sexual, or financial well-being.

For the health niche, the desire could be to lose weight, lower your blood pressure, build muscle, etc. For the biz op space, it could be to work from home, quit your job, etc. And for the financial space, where I operate, it could be safety in retirement or taking care of family.

The New Mechanism

Once your readers believe your new opportunity is the key to their desire, now they must believe you're the only one who can meet that need. You have to make them believe that ONLY your new mechanism can help them.

Having a new mechanism is key in today's competitive market environment. No matter what niche you operate in, chances are your prospects have seen everything. Remember the wise words of Eugene Schwartz:

"If your market is at the stage where they've heard all the claims, in all their extremes, then mere repetition or exaggeration won't work any longer. What this market needs now is a new device... a new mechanism, a new way to make the old promise work. A fresh chance, a brand-new possibility of success where only disappointment has resulted before."

While the new opportunity reveals WHAT is unique about your solution, the new mechanism reveals HOW it works. It's the vehicle that deliver the new opportunity. It's the secret sauce that explains why your solution works.

In the financial niche, it could be the proprietary algorithm behind the strategy/trading system you're selling.

In the biz op space, it could be a mentorship program about a new type of online business.

In the health niche, it could be a unique combination of natural herbs in just one pill, which is very common in supplement offers.

Once you know your new opportunity, your customer's desire, and your new mechanism, you're ready to write down your one belief.

Here are a Few Examples of "The One Belief"

The one belief for P-90X:

Avoiding the plateau effect (new opportunity) is the key to building muscle (desire) and it's attainable only through the P90-X "muscle confusion" system (new mechanism).

The one belief for Jeff Walker's Product Launch Formula:

Warming up your prospects (new opportunity) is the key to successfully launching a new product online (desire) and it's attainable only through the Jeff Walker's Product Launch Formula (new mechanism).

The one belief for Proactive:

Attacking acne at every stage of the cycle (new opportunity) is the key to keeping your skin clear and healthy-looking (desire) and it's attainable only through Proactiv's Combination Therapy® (new mechanism).

The one belief for Invisalign:

Aligning your teeth without ugly braces (new opportunity) is the key to getting the smile you want without disrupting your life (desire) and it's attainable only through the Invisalign proprietary technology (new mechanism).

The one belief for Subway (before Jared got arrested for child pornography):

Eating healthy fast food (new opportunity) is the key to losing weight (desire) and it's attainable only through a diet based on Subway sandwiches (new mechanism).

The one belief for water pitcher Turapur:

Drinking ionized water (new opportunity) is the key to feeling young and energetic (desire) and it's attainable only through Turapur Pitcher's unique filtering system (new mechanism).

The one belief for Febreze:

Adding a pleasant smell at the end of your cleaning routine (new opportunity) is the key to keeping your home looking fresh and clean (desire) and it's attainable only through Febreze's OdorClear technology (new mechanism.)

The one belief for three different financial offers I wrote:

Getting in the trade before the news is published (new opportunity) is the key to making easy money every week (desire) and it's attainable only through the patent-pending Weekly Paycheck Indicator (new mechanism).

Trading penny stocks on Friday (new opportunity) is the key to making easy money every weekend (desire) and it's attainable only through Tim Sykes's proprietary news screen system (new mechanism).

Investing in private companies before they go public (new opportunity) is the key to making the biggest gains in the stock market (desire) and it's attainable only through the secret IPO account I uncovered (new mechanism).

And here's the one belief for my copy method:

Following a copy system that provides clarity, purpose, and structure (new opportunity) is the key to writing converting copy in no time (desire) and it's attainable only through the 16-word sales letter™ (new mechanism).

I could go on and on. But the truth of the matter is you could write the one belief for every single successful marketing campaign throughout history.

So what's the one belief for the project you're working on?

Once you write that down, you can move on to the ten sequential questions. They'll structure the promo for you, making your job way easier.

Chapter 3

Injecting Dopamine into Your Prospect's Brain with Question #1

He was a very quiet kid. He hardly spoke at all until he was three years old. In fact, his parents worried there was something wrong with him.

When he was five years old, his parents gave him a magnetic compass. And that changed everything.

He was fascinated by the fact that no matter which way he turned the compass, the needle always pointed the same direction. That new toy made him wonder about magnetic fields, which got him interested in physics.

That's how his lifetime journey of exploration started. Many years later, he wrote about the compass, saying: "That experience made a deep and lasting impression on me. Something deeper had to be hidden behind things."

The name of the kid? Albert Einstein. Most of us are not geniuses like he was. But we all have that same capacity to be curious about something new. We love novelty.

And that's why the first question you must answer is this:

Question #1: How is this different from everything else I've seen?

You must begin by explaining what the new opportunity is. As I mentioned in the last chapter, if your idea is not unique, it's useless.

Why? Because it will not active dopamine pathways in your prospect's brains. Without the release of dopamine, your customer will just ignore your message.

Cognitive neuroscientists Nico Bunzeck and Emrah Düzel used MRI images to study how the brain reacts to novelty. They found that there's a region of our midbrain called the substantia nigra or ventral segmental area that "lights up" when we see new stuff.

This "novelty center" of our brain is activated only when we come across something completely new. If it's something familiar, it stays dormant.

Here's how Bunzeck and Düzel explain it:

"When we see something new, we see it has a potential for rewarding us in some way. This potential that lies in new things motivates us to explore our environment for rewards. The brain learns that the stimulus, once familiar, has no reward associated with it and so it loses its potential.

"For this reason, only completely new objects activate the midbrain area and increase our levels of dopamine."

Our Brains are Wired for Novelty

If you think about it, that makes perfect sense from an evolutionary point of view. It was exploring new things that led humans to spread around the world. It's how we were able to adapt to all sorts of different environments.

That happened because we evolved from acting on raw instinct alone to identifying new things and learning about them. The fact that our brains release dopamine when we come across novelty probably gave us a great evolutionary advantage.

My buddy Oren Klaff talks about this in his great book *Pitch Anything*. He says: "Attention will be given when information novelty is high and will drift away when information novelty is low."

He goes on to explain how humans survived in the African Savanna by detecting change:

"The only way to survive from one day to the next is detecting change, because trees were not threatening, grass was not threatening, clouds were not threatening unless they moved.

"Things that moved were threatening to our survival and we dedicated most of the 60% to 80% of our brain matter to detecting change. So if you don't characterize things in terms of change, the physical nature of our brain isn't attracted to it."

Here's the bottom line. Only novelty will release the right dose of dopamine that will get your customer into "exploring" mode—that will get them excited enough to keep reading a sales letter to find out more about that "new" thing.

That's how our brains are wired. Nobody can change that. If you ignore that fact, you'll never succeed in copy.

That's why your USP should always be in your headline and at the beginning of your sales letter. The new opportunity needs to feel like a breakthrough. It needs to feel like you just figured something out, and you're revealing what you discovered to the reader.

It could be a new cure, a new way of losing weight, a new way of making money, a new business model, etc.

In the financial niche, I've written about a new law, a new loophole, a new threat, a new prediction, a new discovery, a new conspiracy, a new political scandal, a new trading system, etc.

Here's how I started the first sales letter I wrote using this method (the one that has sold more than $30 mil):

"Hi, I'm Alan Knuckman.

I'll introduce myself fully in just a moment.

But right now I want you to look at this piece of paper I'm holding in my hand.

It's patent application # D0365193.

It was filed with U.S. Patent and Trademark Office to protect the invention of a powerful NEW market indicator...

The ONLY indicator in the world that can tip you off about impending big market news...

BEFORE the news becomes public."

Notice how I begin the letter by explaining why this is different from everything else they've seen in the past. It has to be truly unique. Once you answer that question, your prospect's brain will be filled with dopamine.

Now you can move on to the next question....

Chapter 4

The Man Who Helped Ending World War I with Toilet Paper

At the end of 1914, the British came up with a new plan to defeat Germany: starve the German people into submission through a blockade strategy.

By 1917, only Sweden and a handful of other minor sources on the European continent were selling goods to Germany.

As a result, German soldiers at the front lines weren't getting the food, clothing, and equipment they needed. Hundreds of thousands of German soldiers didn't have boots, socks, or jackets.

That's when the Allies employed Harry Reichenbach, at that time the greatest American advertiser in history. His mission was to figure out a way to persuade German soldiers to surrender.

How do you persuade someone to become a prisoner of war?

After interviewing hundreds of German soldiers in prison camps, Reichenbach made a list of what their biggest desires were. He then wrote a short sales letter based on those big "pain points."

Their direct mail strategy was to drop 45 million of those letters over Germany's lines. The result? German soldiers started surrendering in masses. So much so that it became a capital offense to pick up any pieces of paper on the ground.

Here's what that sales letter offered:

If they surrendered, all German prisoners would be given officer rank. As "prisoners with officer rank," every day they would get bread and meat to eat, cigarettes to smoke, a comb, and 24 sheets of toilet paper (German soldiers had none in the trenches).

This letter worked because it immediately answered the question "what's in it for me?"

And that's our next question in the process.

Question #2: What's in it for me?

My two boys never seem to listen to me when I try telling them what to do. If you have kids, I'm sure you can relate to that. But there's one little trick that never seem to fail.

If I frame my request with "what's in it for them," they will listen to me. Something as simple as "go finish your homework because as soon as you're done, we can go to the park and play soccer" always works.

In the classic book *How to Win Friends and Influence People*, pretty much all of Dale Carnegie's secrets are about focusing on the other person. Want to make people like you? Become genuinely interested in them and talk in terms of their interests.

Use their name because to that person it's the sweetest and most important sound in any language.

Encourage them to talk about themselves. Make them feel important.

Do any of these influence secrets mention yourself? No. It's all about the other person. And your sales letter should be, too, especially at the beginning. That's why the most important word in any sales letter is "You."

Dale Carnegie talks explicitly about how we're all interested in what we want. For that reason, the only way to influence other people is to talk about what they want.

It seems like such an obvious statement. But I've lost count of how many sales letters I've read that don't answer that question within seconds. They go on and on talking about other stuff, and by the time they answer "what's in it for me?", the reader has given up reading the letter a long time ago.

Never forget: people don't have to read your shit.

It's not like they're sitting at home just waiting for you to send them your offer. It's the opposite.

You're most likely disrupting their day. A lot of people are probably reading your stuff on their phone. And that trend will only accelerate in the coming years.

For that reason, they're looking for a reason NOT to read your letter or watch your VSL. If you don't answer this question within seconds, you're giving them that reason. They'll leave your page and go back to whatever they were doing before.

So put yourself in your customer's shoes and ask yourself "what promise can I make here at the beginning of my letter that will get my customer salivating?"

The big promise must be tied to your customer's key desires.

In the health space, it could be "lose up to 20 pounds a month eating nothing but donuts and pizza."

In the biz op space it could be "make $10,000 a month online without having to build a website, hire a copywriter, or even develop a product."

And here's a section of one of my sales letters with the big promise: "I call it the "weekly paycheck indicator" because it gives you the chance to collect a BIG Paycheck of $10,200 or more... Every. Single. Week."

Make that big promise in the first page of your letter. Because that will probably be the only chance you'll have to make an emotional impact.

We've all heard about the study showing that people today have attention spans shorter than a goldfish's and that we lose focus after eight seconds. I don't know how accurate that number is. But the undeniable truth is that our attention span or patience for irrelevant details is lower than ever.

That's because we're bombarded every day with so much information that we must ignore most of it and focus only on what matters to us. And we tend to do that very, very quickly.

And that's why it's important to answer the question very quickly. In my sales letters, I like to answer both questions #1 and #2 in the first page.

Once you tell your customer how your idea is unique and the big promise it can deliver, you've piqued their interest.

Now you just have to prove you're not full of shit.

And that bring us to the next question....

Chapter 5

In a World Full of Bullshit, Proof

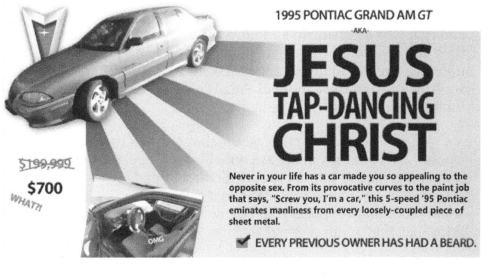

1995 PONTIAC GRAND AM *GT*

·AKA·

JESUS TAP-DANCING CHRIST

Never in your life has a car made you so appealing to the opposite sex. From its provocative curves to the paint job that says, "Screw you, I'm a car," this 5-speed '95 Pontiac eminates manliness from every loosely-coupled piece of sheet metal.

☑ EVERY PREVIOUS OWNER HAS HAD A BEARD.

~~$199,999~~
$700
WHAT?!

OMG

is King

Check out this ad for a 1995 Pontiac found on Craigslist. "Never in your life has a car made you so appealing to the opposite sex." WOW. The landscape is so competitive these days that the only way you can grab someone's attention is by having a ridiculous promise like this one.

For example, in the competitive financial niche, the promises have become more and more ridiculous in the last few years. Doubling your money in one year used to be a good promise.

Now you have to promise doubling your money every day to stand out. Everything needs to be bigger, faster, easier... or you'll have no chance of competing with all the other aggressive promises out there.

Eugene Schwartz talks about this trend of one-upmanship in *Breakthrough Advertising*:

"If a competitor has just introduced a new mechanism to achieve the same claim as that performed by your product, and that new mechanism announcement is producing sales, then you counter in this way. Simply elaborate or enlarge upon the successful mechanism. Make it easier, quicker, surer; allow it to solve more of the problem: overcome old limitations; promise extra benefits."

The problem with this race is that eventually we all hit a point where our promises are unbelievable. And that's why, if you're operating in a competitive market—and these days everyone is—you must follow the first two questions with some proof that supports your one belief. That's why the third question in our method is...

Question #3: How do I know this is real?

If you've done your job right on the previous two questions, your prospect will be pretty skeptical at this point. If you don't show some proof that you can deliver on your promise, they might leave your page. They'll want to believe you because you've made such a good promise. But they'll be skeptical anyway.

So you'll want to show some initial proof, such as historical charts, testimonials, third party quotes, etc. I'm not going to get into the different types of proofs. There are plenty of other copywriting courses and books that talk about them.

Here's what's really important: whatever proof you end up using, you should wrap it up in an ABT structure.

What's an ABT structure? It's a simple story-telling format.

A lot of copywriters show proof **and** more proof **and** more proof, **but** they never create a story around those proof elements. **Therefore**, their sales letters become boring to read and fail to convert prospects into customers.

And there you have it. I just used the ABT structure, which stands for "And" "But" "Therefore."

In the book *Houston, We Have a Narrative: Why Science Needs Story*, author Randy Olson talks about how this ABT idea came from Trey Parker, co-creator of *South Park*.

In a documentary about the show, Parker has explained how he edits the scripts: "I sort of always call it the rule of replacing "and" with either "but" or "therefore"... this happens, THEREFORE this happens, BUT this happens."

Isn't that brilliant? So simple, and so brilliant.

If you think about it, these three little words are the basic building blocks of any narrative.

"And" helps set up the background and give momentum to the story. "But" creates conflict, adding the tension any good story needs. And "therefore" gives the story a conclusion.

No wonder Hollywood screenwriters often follow that format when writing their logline maker, a short description of the concept.

Here's an example of a logline: A young man meets a crazy scientist and travels to the past in a time machine and meets his future parents. But he accidently distracts his mother from noticing and falling in love with his father. Therefore, he is forced to bring them together or he will cease to exist.

Notice that whatever follows after "but" is what really makes the story good. It's all about the tension.

This ABT format is effective because we are hardwired for storytelling. Just like our brains are wired to pay attention to new things, they're also wired to receive information in the ABT format.

A Copy Lesson from Rokia

In 2004, researchers at Carnegie Mellon University conducted a study to see what sorts of messaging compelled people to donate to a charity called Save the Children.

Half the study participants were given the story of Rokia, a little girl in Mali growing up in extreme poverty. She often goes days without food, and her family can't afford basic needs such as healthcare and education.

The other half of the participants were given a letter with all the facts and statistics on poverty in Africa. Those who saw Rokia's story donated an average of $2.38. Those who saw the facts donated an average of $1.14.

But here's the interesting part. They ran the study again, but this time they gave one group both, the story and the facts. They expected that having all the information would boost donations.

But they were wrong. The people in that group donated an average of $1.43, still lower than the story alone. Why did that happen?

As Chip and Dan Heath explain in *Made to Stick, Why Some Ideas Survive and Others Die:* "The researchers theorized that thinking about statistics shifts people into a more analytical frame of mind. When people think analytically, they're less like to think emotionally."

Isn't that fascinating? Give people only facts, and they'll think analytically.

If you're writing a sales letter, that's the last thing you want. That's why it's important when you answer question #3 to use storytelling.

This ABT story format will get your reader to act emotionally, which is exactly what you want.

For example, in the financial niche you can turn even a boring chart with an indicator into an ABT format story with something like this:

"The company had 'sell' ratings... **and** earnings were declining.... Most people thought the company was going bankrupt.... No wonder shares were tanking, as you can see in the chart.

But then out of the blue my indicator flashed a buy signal, indicating shares were about to explode higher. At first nothing happened. I thought the indicator had failed.

But as soon as the market opened the next day, boom, shares exploded higher. **So (therefore)** had you placed a simple trade, you could have made a quick $9,500 that day."

Here's another example from another sales letter I wrote. Notice how the "but" in this lead adds a lot of intention to the story. In all these years, he (the guru of this newsletter) never wrote a letter to the President. But now he had no choice. He had to do it.

At this point of this lead, the reader is thinking "this must be a big deal." It builds so much tension into the lead that the reader has no choice but to keep reading to find out what's happening... and why he wrote this letter.

"In the next 60 seconds I'm going to show you an urgent letter I've just written to President Trump.

You see, I've spent the last 40 years advising top government officials...

In the late 1990s, for example, I worked with members of the Federal Reserve bank to save America from a $1.3 trillion banking crisis.

It would have imploded the US economy. But thanks to my work, it never happened.

After 9/11, I started working with senior military leaders at the Pentagon and the highest ranks of the CIA.

And helped them develop a financial model to predict the next 9/11... by analyzing unusual activity in airline stocks.

A few years later, in 2007, I delivered a message to the US Treasury.

Warning them the housing collapse was about to get a whole lot worse.

But in all those years...

And despite all those threats to our nation...

I never had to write a letter to the president of the United States...

Until today!

Take a look...

[note: I showed the image of the letter in the copy]

I recently wrote this letter to President Trump...

Warning him about what I expect to happen as early as July 1st, 2018...

And I want to share my findings with you today...

Because thanks to this event...

You now have a small retirement window.

If you're older than 60, the next 120 days will be critical for you...

Take the right steps, and you could secure a comfortable retirement in 2018.

If you do nothing during that small window of opportunity...

I'm afraid you'll NEVER be able to retire comfortably."

If you're writing sales letters in the health space, instead of just citing scientific results, try to tell the story of the scientific discovery.

Here's an example from a successful health promotion written by Paul Amos, one of the best in the business:

"In the 1930s and 1940s, Dr. Warburg's experiments on cellular respiration... the way our cells use oxygen for energy... revealed something ASTONISHING.

In order to survive, cancer cells function in a way <u>completely unlike</u> that of regular cells.

They actually use a different cellular 'fuel' than healthy cells normally use...

And if you simply 'shut off' this fuel supply, <u>cancer cells die</u>.

But because regular cells don't have to use this 'fuel'... *they aren't affected at all.*

The cancer cells die... almost immediately... and regular cells continue to stay healthy."

Can you see how this is way more effective than just citing a boring scientific paper? A narrative is always much more engaging than simply listing data, facts, and findings.

Here's a different way of thinking about this. Imagine you're talking to your prospect through a two-way radio. Your prospect is always on the storytelling channel. If you're just citing facts, he won't get your message. You must be on the same channel.

Remember, your mission is to make the reader believe in the one belief. So the entire purpose of presenting proof in an ABT format is to help make your customer believe. Once you have some proof, you can move to the next question...

And that's where the magic really happens!

Chapter 6

It's Time to Reveal the REAL Problem with Question #4

Imagine trying to sell a product in the healthy diet space with the following copy:

"If you're struggling to lose weight, it's probably because your diet is based on bagels, donuts, and pizza... and you never go to the gym."

Or imagine trying to sell a financial newsletter with this:

"If you haven't saved enough for retirement, it's probably because you're bad with money and didn't start saving early enough."

Or this one in the biz op space:

"If you haven't launched your own online business, it's probably because you're afraid of failing and not really the entrepreneur type."

Think any of these pieces of copy would have any chance of success? Hell no. That's not what people want to hear.

In general, people don't want to take responsibility for their failures. If you want to sell more, you need to justify their failures.

As Blair Warren wrote in *The One Sentence Persuasion Course* (my favorite copywriting book of all time):

"While millions cheer Dr. Phil as he tells people to accept responsibility for their mistakes, **millions more are looking for someone to take the responsibility off their shoulders**. To tell them that they are not responsible for their lot in life.

"And while accepting responsibility is essential for gaining control of one's own life, assuring others they are not responsible is essential for gaining influence over theirs."

And that's why the next question you must answer is...

Question #4: What's holding me back?

The purpose of this question is to justify your prospect failure by revealing the REAL PROBLEM.

When your prospects hit the sales page, many of them have already tried numerous similar products.

In the financial niche, maybe they've tried several different investment strategies.

In the health niche, maybe they've tried multiple weight loss products or plans.

Most of those probably didn't work for them. Maybe they've lost money with other financial newsletters. Or maybe they've tried a supplement or a workout plan and didn't lose any weight.

Whatever the situation, it's important to realize they've probably tried something similar in the past.

We need to justify their failure by showing them the REAL reason why those strategies or products they've tried in the past have not worked.

And here's where the simplicity of this copy method comes in. In order to find the real problem, all you need to do is reverse-engineer your answer to question #1.

I know this may sound confusing. Let me walk you through a real example using one of my sales letters.

This particular promo was selling a financial indicator that could help you get in a trade before market-moving news was published. The answer to question #1 (How is this unique?) for that sales letter was this:

It's the only indicator in the world that helps you get in the trade BEFORE the news is published.

Now, here's question #4: What's holding me back?

Answer: The real problem is that you're getting in the trade AFTER the news is published. By the time you get in it's already too late and the big gains have already been made.

See how simple this can be? It's simple, but very powerful. You're telling your customers the reason why they failed in the past is that all the solutions they tried never addressed the REAL problem. But now there's finally a NEW OPPORTUNITY, a new solution that addresses the real problem.

It's All About Giving Your Prospect Hope

Your prospects will think this could finally be what they've been looking for. This won't fail like everything else they've tried in the past.

You're essentially giving them hope. And isn't that what we're all really selling?

That's why I said before that this is where the magic happens. Without hope, your prospect will not buy. And the good news is that you can use this in any niche.

In fact, this is very common in the health space, where you'll see things like "if you're working out and eating healthy, but you're still struggling to lose weight... it's not your fault. It's because your testosterone levels are low/ your thyroid isn't working/ you have bad bacteria in your gut, [insert the real problem here]...."

You're revealing the real problem, a problem that can be solved only by your new mechanism. Of course, all this needs to be based on solid logic and backed up by facts.

Here's how I did it in that financial offer I mentioned before:

"If you've lost money with other indicators or trading systems in the past... it's NOT your fault.

That's because all other systems on earth that I'm aware of are based on price data.

They only trigger a 'buy' signal when the price changes... AFTER the big moves.

By the time you get in, it's already too late.

The breakthrough indicator you're about to see is totally different....

It's a brand new way of making money.

It's all about getting AHEAD of everyone else...

And collecting a BIG paycheck when the information finally becomes public.

That's why it's protected by U.S. Patent Application # D0365193."

See how I took the blame of their failures off their shoulders and put it onto the old opportunities they tried?

That's how you plant the seeds of hope in your prospects' minds. You're starting to tell them, indirectly, that they've failed because they didn't have what you're offering.

And FINALLY you're giving them the opportunity to replace what's not working with something better: your new mechanism.

At this point your prospects will begin to believe that your new mechanism is the only thing that can help them achieve what they desire (a key part of the one belief).

You've justified your prospects' failures and given them hope. Now we're going to inject even more emotion into your sales letter by leveraging your prospects' tribal instincts.

Chapter 7

It's Time to Play the "Us vs. Them" Card with Question #5

"The end of Earth is near. You need to leave the planet now by boarding a spaceship that's trailing the Hale-Bopp Comet. But in order to enter that spaceship, you must abandon your human body.

All you need to do is eat this apple sauce mixed with lethal doses of phenobarbital. But don't worry. An unidentified flying object (UFO) will take your soul to another level of existence above human."

What would you do if I told you that? Probably put me in a straitjacket, right?

But in 1997, 38 people believed every word of that and followed those directions, in a mass suicide by the Heaven's Gate cult.

As a copywriter, I find this very interesting. I'm just trying to persuade people to give me their credit card number. And here you have a cult leader who convinced 38 people that committing suicide would enable them to enter a spaceship flying in the wake of a comet.

Don't you want to know his persuasive secrets?

Well, one of the secrets of this cult (and every cult) is that cult leaders make their members feel like they're part of a special group. They isolate members from friends and family by convincing them that those outside the cult just don't get it.

That's why Scientology (yes, it's a cult!) advocates something they call "disconnection" as key to their members' spiritual growth. What is disconnection? It's basically cutting all ties to anyone who criticizes scientology, including family and friends.

But this type of group dynamic doesn't happen only in cults. Our brains are wired to be tribal. According to psychological studies, any group of humans will sort themselves into us/them groups within seconds, and for almost any reason.

One study has shown that a 50-millisecond exposure to the face of someone of another race is enough to activate the amygdala. Another study has shown that fans at a soccer match are more likely to aid an injured spectator if he's wearing the home team jersey.

My favorite is a study showing how this happens at the subconscious level, proving that "us vs. them" happens automatically.

This study involved morning commuters at a train station in a predominantly white neighborhood. They filled out questionnaires about their political views. Then at half the stations, a pair of Mexicans began to appear each morning chatting quietly in Spanish before boarding the train.

After two weeks, commuters filled out a second questionnaire. The presence of the Mexicans speaking Spanish made people more supportive of decreasing LEGAL immigration from Mexico and making English the official language. Fascinating, right?

If you think about it from the point of view of evolution, it makes a lot of sense. Our caveman ancestors survived only by being part of a group. The group provided comfort and protection against rival groups and the challenging environment.

Nobody is immune to this need to be part of a group.

There are many ways to make people feel like they're part of a group. But having a common enemy is one of the most powerful ways.

That's why the "us vs. them" card is so powerful. We've seen its power throughout history in some of the most memorable conflicts.

Conquistadors vs. Natives in the 16th century.

Christians vs. Muslims during the Crusades.

American Colonies vs. the British Empire during the American Revolution.

North vs. South during the American Civil War.

Nazi Germans vs. Jews before and during WWII.

Capitalism vs. socialism during the Cold War.

Jihadists vs. "Infidels" in acts of terrorism that continue through today.

Back in 2001, I personally experienced this "us vs. them" mentality. In the immediate aftermath of the 9/11 attacks, America came together. The nation was united as one. Stores ran out of flags, millions donated blood, thousands enlisted.

At the time, I was an international student trying to learn English in Nebraska. The day after the attack, I was in one my classes when a discussion about immigration began. One of the students proclaimed: "Why do we even allow these international students here? We should just kick them out."

At that time, I couldn't comprehend why anyone would say something dumb like that, especially a college student. But now I know he was just putting me in the "them" bucket. If I wasn't an American, I must have been one of "them."

That comment wasn't coming from his frontal cortex. It was coming from his reptilian brain. I'm sure you've experienced us vs. them too. We all have. We see it in our day-to-day lives... your favorite team vs. the other teams, Democrats vs. Republicans, dog lovers vs. cat lovers, etc.

Science shows that having a common enemy releases oxytocin, increasing the sense of belonging. And guess what? If you make your prospects feel like part of a group, they'll be more inclined to buy your product. No wonder some of the most successful ads set someone or something up as a common enemy.

Just look at what most critics rank as one of the best ads of all time, the iconic 1984 ad for Apple's first Macintosh. In that ad, PC users are portrayed as gray, mindless drones blindly taking direction from a Big Brother-like character.

Then enters a young, fit, and attractive woman (representing Apple) who is heroic enough to smash the giant screen. Or how about the more recent ads featured the PC guy (wearing a suit and looking like a nerd) and the "Mac," looking cool and competent?

That's how Apple created an enemy, the PC and its users. And they built that common enemy into much of their marketing. No wonder Apple has created an obsessive brand loyalty.

The bottom line is that having a common enemy will do wonders for your sales letter. And that's why it's the next step in the process.

In the previous question, we revealed the real reason why your prospect has failed so far. Now it's time to blame someone or something for that. And we do that by answering the following question...

Question #5: Who/What is to Blame?

In order to find an effective enemy, you must understand your prospect. Instead of trying to create an enemy out of the blue, you must leverage existing beliefs.

For example, most financial newsletter buyers are conservatives who distrust the media and Wall Street and, of course, despise Democrats and liberals. For that reason, Obama, Hillary, Democrats, Wall Street bankers, and the biased media have all been effectively used as a common enemy.

In the anti-aging supplement niche, a lot of the prospects are older people who already believe prescription costs are out of control. Naturally, it's common to set up greedy pharmaceutical companies as the enemy.

Here's how I set up the rigged game on Wall Street as the common enemy in one of my sales letters:

"Remember that famous line from the movie *Wall Street*...

When trader Gordon Gecko said...

'You're either on the inside or the outside.'

Well, everyday investors like you and me have always been 'on the outside'...

I'm sure you've noticed this too, right?

Only insiders with access to special information were able to profit from those BIG one-day moves.

The little guy was simply left out of those big gains.

That rigged-game ends today...."

And here's how I set up the mainstream media as the common enemy in another letter that was selling a cryptocurrency masterclass:

"While I was telling everyone Bitcoin would succeed....

The mainstream media was saying the exact opposite.

Business Insider called Bitcoin "something strange." And they questioned "why anyone would think it's useful."

CNN said it was "a big scam designed to enrich its shadowy creators" and "a bubble that could soon pop."

And the Slate published an article with the headline "Bitcoin is a Ponzi scheme—the Internet's favorite currency will collapse."

Well, had you ignored the clueless mainstream media...

And listened to what I said on CNBC instead...

You would be up 3,710% today.

That's more than 38 times your money in the last four years...

Enough to turn a small retirement account of 10 grand into a $381,044 retirement fortune!

Bottom line...

Don't expect the mainstream media to show you how to make a fortune from new tech trends, including digital currencies.

Because they're always late to the party.

Without my 3-step script, they're totally lost.

Not to mention that there's a lot of misinformation out of there...

Some of my followers are getting scammed into investing in the wrong cryptocurrencies.

That's why I've made my mission to reveal the TRUTH about making money in this booming market."

Once you inject more emotion into your copy by attacking a common enemy, it's time to give them a strong reason to act right now.

Let's take a page from Hitler's book.

Chapter 8

The One Sentence that Killed as Many as 21 Million People

"Either the German people annihilate the Jews or the Jews will enslave them." Adolf Hitler

This one sentence killed millions of people. Yes, Hitler was a monster. He was also a master persuader. Did you ever stop to think how he convinced an entire nation to slaughter as many as 21 million people during his brutal 12-year Third Reich?

He applied several persuasion techniques in his speeches, like the one you see above. This powerful technique is known as the "either-or" fallacy. It's a sentence that drastically raises the stakes by creating a false dilemma in the mind of the audience.

By using that technique, Hitler made Germans believe they had no other option. They had to kill Jews. There was no compromise.

As a result, that sentence created an incredible sense of urgency among Germans. They had to act.

If this technique can make 70 million rational people engage in horrible atrocities, imagine what it could do your sales letter.

That's why the next question in the process is designed to create a false dilemma in the mind of your prospect with the "either-or" technique.

Here's the question...

Question #6: Why Now?

Studies show that whenever you try to persuade someone, you'll face four levels of resistance from your prospect.

The first one is reactance. That happens when your prospect feels like you're trying to limit their freedom to choose or act. Nobody likes losing their freedom. That's why high-pressure sales techniques often backfire.

And it's why it's often a bad idea to mention your product in the lead of your sales letter. Because if your prospects get even a whiff that you're trying to sell something, there's a high chance they'll close that page.

Just think about it... how do you feel when a salesperson rings your doorbell, and the moment you open the door they ask you: "Would you like to buy...?" Before they finish the sentence, you already want to slam the door in their face, right? That's reactance.

The second level of resistance is distrust. And that means your prospect will be skeptical of any claims you make. We've already discussed how to overcome that with question #3.

As you'll see in the next chapter, Question #7 will also help destroy this persuasion barrier.

The third level is scrutiny. Your prospect will need to see proof. We all know that people buy on emotion and justify their emotional decision with logic. That's scrutiny. As you'll see later in this book, Question #8 is designed to break that barrier.

Finally, another face of resistance is inertia. You can make an incredible promise with tons of proof. But that's still not enough to make your prospect buy. That's because of inertia. Staying put is a lot easier than acting on something. We simply tend to resist change.

And that's where "why now?" comes in.

We need to start planting the seeds in your prospect's head that he's facing an "either-or" situation. Either you act now, or you'll miss out on this incredible opportunity. Either you act now, or you could lose everything.

The key here is to raise the stakes. Just having a date as a deadline is not enough. You need to trigger FOMO in your prospect.

You can start doing that in the lead, and throughout the promo, especially in the offer section. After teasing an urgent event on October 26 in one of my sales letters, here's how I revealed the details and raised the stakes:

"In fact, I want you to mark October 26 on your calendar...

Because this single event is about to catapult cryptocurrencies into the third and most explosive stage of the boom.

I am certain that Amazon WILL ACCEPT Bitcoin.

They have no choice. And this will be the tipping point that will create massive generational wealth unlike we've ever seen before.

Given the company's history of staying ahead of its retail rivals...

Amazon could make the announcement as early as October 26, at 4 p.m., during its next earnings conference call.

Which is why you need to act RIGHT NOW.

Once they make this announcement, the impact on cryptocurrencies will be huge.

We'll see a buying frenzy like never before.

It'll be like a Black Friday crowd at Best Buy.

Only those who get in early will get a good deal.

Most people will be left out.

That's why I urge you to get in right now...

Get ahead of the crowd...

Ahead of the massive buying frenzy that will push cryptocurrencies straight up."

See how I used the "either-or" technique to create massive urgency? Either you get in now, ahead of this big event, or you won't make any money.

For your next project, think about how you can use this lesson from Hitler to destroy inertia and get your prospect to act.

We've covered a lot of ground so far, so let's recap a bit. At this point, your prospects have been presented with a new opportunity. You've shown evidence that this is real. You've justified your prospects' failure and established a common enemy. And you've teased why they must act now.

But remember, distrust is one of the psychological barriers. Now it's time to show them why they should trust you.

Chapter 9

How to Make Your Prospect Know, Trust, and Like You

Secretary: "Pan American airlines, can I help you?"

Frank: "Yes ma'am, I'd like to speak with someone in the purchasing department."

Secretary: "One moment please"

Clerk: "How can I help you?"

Frank: "My name is John Black. I'm a co-pilot with the company, based out of San Francisco. I've been with the company seven years and I've never had something like this come up before."

Clerk: "What's the problem?"

Frank: "Well, we flew in yesterday and we're going out today. Yesterday, I sent my uniform to my hotel to have it dry cleaned. Now the hotel and the cleaner said they can't find it. And I have to flight in 4 hours."

Clerk: "Don't you have a spare uniform?"

Frank: "Certainly, back home in San Francisco, but I'd never get it in time for my flight"

Clerk: "Hold on...."

A few minutes later...

Clerk: "My supervisor says you need to go down to the Well-Built Uniform Company on 5th Avenue. They're our supplier. I'll call them and let them know you're on the way."

And that's how Frank Abagnale was able to get a Pan Am uniform, even though he couldn't fly a kite, let alone an airplane.

If you've read the book or watched the movie *Catch Me if You Can*, you know the story. Pan Am estimates that between the ages of 16 and 18, Frank flew more than 1 million miles for free, boarded more than 250 commercial airlines and traveled to 26 countries around the world. He never once stepped onboard a Pan Am aircraft.

Instead, he abused the professional courtesy of other airlines to provide free transport for competing airline pilots if they had to move to another city at short notice. He only pulled this off because of that uniform. It gave him instant authority, just like white lab coats give doctors authority. It made people trust that he was a pilot with the airline.

And that's why authority is one of the key elements of persuasion, as you probably already know from Robert Cialdini's classic book.

And that's why the next question in the process is this...

Question #7: Why should I trust you?

This will be the credibility section of your sales letter. There are three main "storylines" I've found that work best to establish authority and make your prospect trust and like you.

The first and most powerful one is the "I've been in your shoes" storyline. Then there are the Robin Hood and the expert storylines.

Let's take a look at each one.

The "I've been in your shoes" Storyline

The goal here is to show your prospect that you (the guru, editor, etc.) went through the same challenges your prospect is facing right now. That at some point everything seemed lost. But then you discovered your new mechanism, and it changed everything. It helped you overcome all the challenges and achieve the same things your prospect desires.

This is powerful because you're indirectly talking about your prospect's deepest desires through your own story. You're painting the picture of how their life could be. But you're doing it in a very indirect way that will trigger no resistance from your prospect.

By telling your journey, your reader will think "OMG, this guy is just like me. Finally, someone who gets it. That's exactly what I'm going through right now. And he already achieved what I want." How can your prospect not trust that?

Here's how I did that in one of my sales letters that offered a penny stock advisory service.

I knew most of my prospects were frustrated with slow-moving stocks and not making much money with those "safe" stocks. I also knew most of them came from middle-class families. To make this even more powerful, I also added a testimonial/case study towards the end to show that anybody can do this.

Here's the copy:

"You see, when I started investing...

I traded expensive, blue chip stocks because that's what everyone told me you had to do to get rich in the long run.

But those stocks move way too slow. My portfolio didn't move an inch for months at a time.

So I started trading penny stocks....

And I started making 20%, 40%, 50% or more in profits... in a matter of days.

I also didn't start with a lot of money.

I grew up as a middle-class kid in a small rural town in Connecticut.

I wasn't born with a silver spoon in my mouth.

So penny stocks were perfect for someone like me... who wasn't rich yet.

But WANTED to get rich.

That's the beauty of penny stocks....

You can start with very little money because they trade for pennies on the dollar....

And because they're so explosive, you can make a fortune fast.

Look what happened to Tim Gritanni....

When he started following my strategy a few years ago....

He was selling insurance for State Farm... and he only had $1,500 to his name.

Today he's a multimillionaire."

The Robin Hood Storyline

As you know, the folkloric hero Robin Hood is a noble outlaw in Sherwood Forest who fights the oppressive evil of King John by robbing from the rich and giving to the poor. In this storyline, you will be "stealing" a secret from the rich and giving it to the reader.

This works even better if you accidently stumbled into a secret "they didn't want you to know." And now for the first time ever you're blowing the whistle to level the playing field.

Here's something I've used in one of my sales letters:

"I've spent most of my adult life trading derivatives on Wall Street.

As a 22-year old kid, I was already trading $100 million accounts....

After that, the stakes only got higher.

At one point, I was personally making millions of dollars per year...

Going on annual ski trip to Switzerland, where I stayed at billionaire Richard Branson's chalet...

Attending lavish events, like the Grand Prix in Monaco... even the *Kill Bill* premiere in Cannes.

If you've watched the movie *The Wolf of Wall Street*, you get the idea.

But no matter how much money I made...

I wasn't happy working on Wall Street.

Helping the rich getting richer and watching bankers screw the little guy wasn't fulfilling.

So after years of seeing the rotten machine from the inside...

I had finally had enough...

And decided to leave everything behind.

But here's what's important...

When I left Wall Street I took an income secret with me...

One that I've never revealed to anyone until today...."

The Expert Storyline

If you can't use "I've been in your shoes" or Robin Hood storylines, then your next best option is to position your main character as a guru by talking about his expertise. That includes books, TV appearances, experience, or any accomplishments that proves expertise in the field.

Here's an example from one of my sales letters:

"I started my trading career in 1991, when I joined the Chicago Board of Trade right out of college.

And I've spent the last 25 years on the trading floor...

Working through the ranks... from being a runner, phone clerk and broker...

All the way up to becoming a professional trader...

And a member of the Chicago Board of Trade...

Where I traded my own account on the floor...

And competed with the world's best traders.

You might have seen me on Bloomberg, CNBC, Fox Business, and other major financial news...

Where I'm frequently invited to share my views on the market."

These storylines are not mutually exclusive. You can mix and match them when appropriate to make the story even more powerful. Once your prospect knows, trusts, and likes you, by this point they should be emotionally sold.

I know I've covered a lot of ground so far. But on average I answer all these first seven question in the first 1/3 of the sales letter. Once the emotional sale is done, you're going to help your prospects justify their decision with solid logic.

It's time to show them how your new mechanism actually works.

Chapter 10

How to Make Your Prospect Nod his Head and Think "Yeah, that Makes Sense."

Here's a real conversation between a farmer and a doctor back in the 1920s:

Farmer: "Doc, is there anything you can do for...you know... sexual weakness?"

Doctor: "Sorry, but there's nothing to be done for impotence."

Farmer, after noticing a male goat mounting a female goat through the window: "It's too bad I don't have billy goat nuts. Say, Doc! Why don't you just put some goat nuts in me? Graft 'em on, like the way I graft Pound Sweet on an apple stray!"

Doctor: "Are you serious?"

Farmer: "Well, Doc, they can't be worse than the nuts I got. Just give it a try, and if it don't work, I sure as heck won't tell nobody."

And that's how one of the most bizarre stories in quackery began. If you've read the great book from Dan Kennedy, *Make Them Believe*, you know the Brinkley story.

According to Dr. John Brinkley, that farmer's wife gave birth to a healthy baby boy nine months after the goat testicle transplant. The boy was named Billy (after the goat).

Goat testicle transplant. Talk about a brand-new mechanism. This worked because farmers (Dr. Brinkley's primary prospects) already believed goats were sexual dynamos. It was an accepted fact.

Heck, to this date, many people still believe that. It's why eating penises and testicles from donkeys, goats, and bulls is popular in certain parts of Asia.

Without that existing belief, Dr. Brinkley would probably have never pulled this off. Even though there was no scientific proof that his method worked, whenever he explained the mechanism, his prospects went "yeah, that makes sense."

He channeled an existing belief (goats are sexual dynamos) to support what would otherwise be a ridiculous claim.

And that's your goal in this next step of the copy. You have to answer this next question in a way that will make your prospects nod their heads.

Here's the question...

Question #8: How does it work?

It's time to reveal how your new mechanism actually works. If you can do that by exploring an existing belief (like Dr. Brinkley did), it will make your copy stronger.

Now, we're not farmers back in the 1920s. Your prospects are a lot smarter now. Aside from exploring an existing belief, you better be able to explain your mechanism in a very logical way... in a way that will make you reader think "oh yeah, that makes total sense."

Your prospect needs to understand exactly how your new mechanism gives him the end result you're promising. The key here is to remember that this proof and the explanation of your mechanism are also copy. As such, they cannot be boring.

That's a mistake I see many writers making. Remember, if you wrap the explanation of the mechanism in an ABT storytelling frame, your copy will be much easier for the reader to consume.

Here's how I answered that question in one of my sales letters that talked about a new tax law that would trigger repatriation of money.

That repatriation was my new mechanism. And I called it the "cash for patriots program." My prospects were conservatives who already believed Trump was trying to do everything he could to "make America great again."

Here's the copy:

"There are literally trillions of dollars at stake.

I'm talking about $27,718 on average for every American taxpayer.

In order to take advantage of this opportunity, it's important that you first understand where all this money is coming from.

The first thing you should know is that it doesn't come from the U.S. government.

Even though this is a government program, the money comes from the private sector.

The Trump administration is simply creating the conditions to unleash $2.6 trillion into the hands of everyday Americans.

You see, because the U.S. dollar is the world's reserve currency...

Other countries around the world also use our currency.

For that reason, there are trillions of dollars circulating outside the U.S.

And the Joint Committee on Taxation (JCT) has identified a stash of $2.6 trillion... mostly hiding in Ireland.

Trump's plan is designed to bring some of the cash back home.

In a recent speech to the Detroit Economic Club he said his administration will 'bring back trillions of dollars that is now parked overseas.'

He believes that's money that belongs to American patriots.

It's part of his 'America comes first' philosophy.

Why leave all the cash outside the U.S. if it can come home and help our citizens?

It's hard to argue with that argument.

In fact, BOTH Democrats and Republicans agree it's a good idea.

As Bloomberg says, '[the cash for patriots program] may be one of the few things Republicans and Democrats can agree on.'"

Notice how I explored an already existing belief. But I also added extra proof with the quotes from Trump himself and Bloomberg, a credible source. There's no way in hell my prospect will read this and think "this makes no sense."

Once you show your prospect how your new mechanism works, they're ready to buy. They're pre-sold.

At this point, you've proven that your new opportunity is the key to what they desire and it's only attainable through your new mechanism.

Now all you need to do is make a no-brainer offer.

Chapter 11

From Flipping Burgers to Becoming the Richest Man Alive... All Thanks to a No-Brainer Offer

His first job was working at McDonald's in the summer, while also helping out his grandfather on his South Texas ranch.

After developing a no-brainer offer, this kid from Albuquerque, New Mexico, went from flipping burgers to becoming richer than Warren Buffet, Bill Gates, and Mark Zuckerberg.

It all started in his garage in 1994, when he read that the web had grown 2,300% in one year. He then made a list of 20 possible products to sell online. At the top of the list? Books.

Yes, I'm talking about founder of Amazon, Jeff Bezos.

Using scale and thin margins to offer unbeatable prices, Amazon seems to be taking over the world. Combine competitive prices with its shopping experience (1-Click checkout and fast doorstep delivery), and you got a no-brainer offer.

Who doesn't want to buy quality products for less money and receive them as fast as possible? With all the value they offer, you'd have to be a moron NOT to shop on amazon.com. The key word here is "value."

And that's where the next question of the process comes in. It's time to make an offer. But not just any offer.

You must answer the following question with a no-brainer offer...

Question #9: How can I get started?

Your goal here is to put together an offer so good (product/service, price, bonuses, guarantee) that will take your copy to a whole other level. In fact, if you can get your offer right, your copy doesn't even have to be top-notch.

As the saying goes, "the product is mightier than the pen." So how can you make a no-brainer offer?

By creating a huge GAP between the value and the price. In order to accomplish that, you can either offer a ton of value or cut the price or do a combo of both.

Many businesses make the mistake of cutting their prices, and they end up making their products look "cheap" ("with such a low price, this can't be good"). They eventually price themselves out of existence.

Have you ever bought anything that was both the best in the industry and also the cheapest? No! You get what you pay for. And that's how your prospect thinks too. So lowering the price reduces the perceived value of your product and can actually reduce sales.

That's why the best option is to focus on increasing the value of your proposition. Lowering the price is for losers. Don't do it.

You can create the perception of value by comparing it with a higher-price product that could provide a similar solution.

For example, a hedge fund that provides a similar strategy would charge you $100,000. That way, you're anchoring the high price, creating the illusion that your offer is a really good deal.

You can also use scarcity (limiting the number of units available) to increase the perceived value and create urgency.

But the best way to add value to your offer is by adding bonus gifts. And I'm not talking about just any bonuses that you slap together without giving it much thought.

Master online marketer Todd Brown talks about the importance of putting together what he calls S.I.N. Offers — superior, irresistible, and no-brainer. Here's how Todd explains the importance of bonuses:

"The right way to construct your offer is to create your premiums specifically for the offer. Premiums should be so good and so valuable… They should demonstrate such exciting, compelling benefits… That your prospects would happily pay money for them!"

Todd says the way you begin the construction of these premiums is by asking yourself…

"What premiums would perfectly complement my main product and add enormous value to the offer?"

Adding a few good bonuses to your offer will drive your value proposition through the roof. And it will allow you to use the value stack technique from Russell Brunson. What's the value stack?

You basically show the value (not the price) of each item you're offering and add them all up. The goal is to show a huge value that will make your final price offer look like a total give away.

For example, when you see that you're getting $23,450 worth of products for only $1,999, it's an offer that's really hard to pass up.

Once you offer a ton of value, then you want to eliminate the risk for your prospect with a money-back guarantee or other type of risk reversal ("it will cost you nothing if you're not happy").

Here's a basic template for an offer that I like to use in my sales letters:

Reveal the special report (the main offer)

Introduce subscription service (you get the report when you join the service)

What others are saying (testimonials for the service)

False Close (Anchor a high price)

Extra Bonuses (Show how each bonus has value)

Value Stack (Show total value)

Final price (Cut the value and reveal final price)

Guarantee (Risk reversal)

Assuming you did everything right up to this point, all you have to do now is finish strong and avoid a big mistake I see a lot of people making in the closing.

Are you making that mistake? Check out the next chapter for the answer.

Chapter 12

It's Time to Close with the Powerful Push-Pull Technique

Here's advice from a famous pickup artist on how to seduce "a legit 10" at a bar:

"Let's say she has long nails which are most likely fake. Now why do 10s dress so FINE if they don't want the attention? Sometimes they LOVE the feeling of control.

They are in a club with friends and they want to be the leader of the circle (social hierarchy in primates) and so she gets all the attention.

The guys come and buy drinks for them and she gets off on knocking the guys down. It's all in a day's play.

Ok, so she is wearing fake nails to look even BETTER! Most guys will say, "Wow you are so beautiful!"

BORING, typical and in her mind by now, TRUE.

Imagine now, a guy comes along and says "Nice nails. Are they real?"

She will have to concede, "No, acrylic."

And he says (like he didn't notice it was a put down), "Oh. (Pause) well I guess they still LOOK good."

Then he turns his back to her."

This comes straight from Mystery, the famous pick-up artist featured in the book *The Game.* Have you ever come across as "too needy" when approaching a girl? I know I have.

And in those cases, my failure rate was 100%. Nobody likes a needy person.

As my buddy Oren Klaff likes to say, "people want what they can't have, they chase what moves away from them, and they only value that which they pay for."

The same way you can turn a hot woman off by being too needy, you can turn your prospect off if you sound too desperate for the sale.

And that's exactly a mistake many copywriters make at the closing.

They're so desperate for those royalties... so desperate to close the sale... so desperate to finally have that blockbuster hit they've been dreaming about... that it shows in the copy.

They're basically begging the prospect to buy. And that's the last thing you want to do in the offer section.

So what should you do? You should take a page from the pickup artist playbook and alternate between attraction and disinterest signals in a push-pull fashion.

First, you're going to push your prospect away by making them feel they're in control. It's their decision. They have options. Maybe this is not even right for them.

Then pull them back in by reminding them of what's at stake. Paint the picture of what they have to lose if they don't act.

It's time to answer the last question of the process...

Question #10: What do I have to lose?

Remember, we started this whole process with the one belief. By now, your prospect either believes it or you have no chance of selling. So remind him how your new opportunity is the key to what he desires and that it's only attainable through your new mechanism.

Then, raise the pain levels by painting the picture of how his life will remain the same if he doesn't act. Whatever problem he has will not be solved. The key here is not to be needy and to let your prospect decide for himself.

Here's how I closed one of my letters:

"Look, you've seen how you could have made weekend profits of $8,780, $9,100 or even $15,820... All by using my simple weekend strategy.

You saw how people who are following my strategy are already making a quick fortune on the weekends...

I've negotiated a special charter membership offer with a one-time $2,000 discount...

With a performance guarantee that fully covers the price of your subscription.

Now it's time for a decision.

The Way I See It You Have Three Options...

Option #1: Do absolutely nothing and stay exactly where you are right now.

If you already have enough to retire and you're not worried about running out of money during your golden years...

Then maybe you don't need this weekend strategy.

But if you'd like to make some extra income on the weekends, that leaves you with two other options...

Option #2: Do it yourself.

You can try to keep track of all the millions of financial news and blog posts that are published every day...

Then try to analyze all the 1,887 stocks that are currently trading below $5...

And hope you'll pick the right one... the one that could pay you a fortune on Monday.

If you're willing to work hard and spend hours in front of your computer, you might be able to pull it off.

Option #3: Let me do the heavy lifting for you

I'll put my proven news filtering system to work for you.

I'll do the legwork and send you my research and video alerts.

All you need to do is read my research and place the trade on a Friday if you decide to invest...

Go enjoy your weekend...

Then come back on Monday to collect your profits.

Of these three options, ask yourself...

What's Going to Be Easier for You?

You see, there are two types of people in this world...

Those who only dream about achieving their financial goals without ever taking any action to make it happen...

And those who are ready to take action when the opportunity presents itself.

Most people will tell you they want to retire rich.

But we both know very few actually make it happen.

It's a natural law of financial wealth....

The classic tale of the willful and the wishful.

Most people will keep dreaming...

While the few who are actually serious about their financial future will take action.

Since you've watched my entire presentation this far, I think you're one of the few special ones...

One of the 250 people I'm looking for.

If I'm right and you're still with me...

I'm ready to send you that email with the subject line: The Weekend Trade that Could Pay You $6,250 Next Monday.

Only you can decide."

Notice how I only presented the options, without trying to convince the prospect which one he should choose. I've created the illusion that he's in control.

Then I painted the picture that nothing would change in his life if he didn't act. But I did that without being needy. Instead, I created the impression that I couldn't care less what he decides to do.

That's how you want to finish the letter. Remember, people chase what moves away from them.

Chapter 13

Putting it All Together

We've reached the end of the road. Even though it seems we covered a lot, this is a very simple process. It's designed to get you thinking before you write a single piece of copy.

In fact, when I mentor writers in my team, I highly encourage them to write down the one belief for the promo idea... and try to answer at least the first seven question with just a couple of lines.

I do that myself with every single promotion I write. And I've found that very helpful. It's a way to map out the entire promotion in 5-10 minutes.

Then all you need to do is research and start writing on the appropriate sections.

Remember the 16-word sales letter™ that helped me sell $120 million+ in the last two years...

"The secret to converting copy is to define the one belief, then answer these ten questions."

Here's the one belief...

This new opportunity is the key to **their desire** and it's attainable only through my **new mechanism**.

Here are the ten questions...

Question #1: How is this different from everything else I've seen?

Question #2: What's in it for me?

Question #3: How do I know this is real?

Question #4: What's holding me back?

Question #5: Who/What is to blame?

Question #6: Why now?

Question #7: Why should I trust you?

Question #8: How does it work?

Question #9: How can I get started?

Question #10: What do I have to lose?

Here's what to do next...

As you know, writing copy is a very complex process. The market is always evolving... new techniques emerge... the environment change.

There's always something new to learn...

Which is why what I've showed you here is just the tip of the iceberg.

If you'd like to stay on top of your game...

Go to www.dailyinsidersecrets.com and sign up for my FREE daily letter...

Where each day my business partner Peter Coyne and I reveal secrets that are working inside a $1.5 billion online marketing giant.

Signing up for my daily email is a great way to stay in touch.

Let me know how the 16-word sales letter™ is working for you. If you're interested in working with me, let me know as well. I'm always looking for talent.

Good luck!

About Evaldo Albuquerque

After getting a degree in Finance, Evaldo joined one of Agora subsidiaries as a research analyst. After four years as an editor, he finally realized copy was the soul of the business and decided to become a copywriter.

He's been writing copy for Agora Financial since 2014.

He was the top seller copywriter in Agora Financial in 2017.

In 2018, he broke Agora's financial record of most sales in a year, with over $80 million in sales. He's now considered one of the best copywriters in the world. He's the copy chief for Paradigm Press (the largest Agora Financial imprint), where he manages a (growing) team of 12 copywriters.

Acknowledgements

I could not have written this book without the support of a handful of people.

Big thanks to Justin Ford, who hired me and introduced me to the Agora world. I never forgot the first thing you taught me: "The secret to great writing is rewriting."

Big thanks to my former boss Erika Nolan. When I decided to learn more about copy, you were 100% behind me and helped me anyway you could.

Big thanks to Oren Klaff and Blair Warren. Both of your books (Pitch Anything and The One Sentence Persuasion) have greatly influenced how I write copy.

Big thanks to my business partner and publisher of Paradigm Press, Peter Coyne. Although you're 10 years younger than me, you've always been an inspiration. Our discussions in your office gave me the clarity I needed to develop my own system and actually put stuff on paper.

Last but not least, big thanks to Joe Schriefer, publisher of Agora Financial. You're the best mentor anyone could ask for. Your friendship and guidance over the last few years is a big, big reason behind my success as a copywriter.

Made in United States
Orlando, FL
25 May 2023

33486379R00061